Resources

by Donna Watson

PEARSON
Scott Foresman
DK

Natural Resources

Did you know that Earth constantly provides supplies that you need? Some of these supplies are the food you eat, the materials you use to build your home, and the air you breathe. Everything people need to live is right here on Earth!

Using Resources

These supplies from Earth are known as natural resources. Natural resources can be living things, such as plants and animals. They can also be nonliving things, such as soil, water, air, and sunlight. Plants and animals could not survive without these nonliving resources.

Air is a resource that living things need in order to breathe. Water is also a resource. Animals and plants need water to live as well.

Natural resources are either renewable or nonrenewable. Renewable resources are materials that nature can make faster than they are used up. They can be replaced. One renewable resource is **solar energy,** or energy from the Sun. Water, oxygen, and soil are other renewable natural resources. Nonrenewable resources are those that humans use faster than they can be naturally replaced.

Soil as a Renewable Resource

Soil can be found on most of Earth's land. Animals such as ants, earthworms, and prairie dogs build their homes in soil. Many kinds of plants also need soil to live. Soil is a nonliving renewable resource.

Soil forms as a result of weathering, erosion, and deposition. These three processes work together to break down rock, move it to a new place, and drop it off.

Plants weather rock as their roots begin to cause cracks.

Plant roots settle into rock.

Rock begins to crack.

Plants grow in the soil.

Rock is weathered further as more plants cause the cracks to become deeper.

Weathering is the process that breaks down rock. Over long periods of time, loose rock on the surface of Earth breaks down into smaller pieces. Water gets into the cracks in rocks. The water freezes and thaws many times. As ice pushes against the sides of the rock, the cracks get bigger. Finally pieces of the rock break apart. Wind carries away the bits of loose rock.

Water also weathers rock below the surface of Earth. The roots of plants dig their way into rock and break it up too. Even very tall mountains are affected by weathering. The small pieces of rock that break off are moved to a new place through erosion. Then they are dropped off in the process of deposition.

The roots of larger plants, such as trees, weather the rocks even more.

Soil Ingredients

Pieces of weathered rock are only one part of what soil is made of. Soil also has decaying plant and animal materials. This decaying material is called **humus.**

Air, minerals, and humus are some nonliving materials in soil. But soil also has living parts. Some animals, such as moles, burrow in soil. Bacteria, fungi, and insects can live in soil. They are very important because they help break down dead organisms. This provides nutrients that plants need.

Different rocks and minerals make up different kinds of soil. The amount of humus in soil affects how it feels. Minerals can affect soil color.

Soil contains many living and nonliving materials.

Kinds of Soil

The decaying remains of plants and animals are found in topsoil, or the upper layer of soil. Topsoil also contains pieces of weathered rock. The layer below topsoil is subsoil. It is made of some soil and small rocks. Bedrock is below subsoil. It is made mostly of rock. Its minerals have an effect on what kind of soil forms.

Clay soil contains the smallest particles. It can be different colors, depending on what it is made of. Silt is soil that has slightly larger particles. It can feel smooth. Sand is soil made of even larger pieces. Sandy soil has pieces of different minerals. Sand contains mostly quartz. But it can also contain mica and other minerals. Sand can be different colors. Some sand is light colored. Sand with pieces of coral in it can be pink. Sand from volcanic rock can be black.

Clay soil is hard.

Silty soil can be moist and fertile.

Water drains easily through sandy soil.

Growing Plants in Soil

Plants need soil with many nutrients. They cannot get the nutrients they need from soil that has too much sand or clay. Water goes right through sandy soil, washing away nutrients. Clay is too hard to allow plant roots to spread out. The best soil for growing plants is a mixture of clay, silt, sand, and humus.

Renewable Soil

The nutrients in soil can be replaced. This means that soil is renewable. Certain crops that farmers plant can replace lost nutrients in soil. Soil itself cannot be replaced as easily as its nutrients. Just a few centimeters of nutrient-rich topsoil are replaced every one thousand years. But a few centimeters of topsoil can wear away in as few as ten years. Because of this, it is important to reduce soil erosion.

Using Soil in Other Ways

You may think soil is good only for growing plants. But it has many other uses! Pieces of pottery are made from clay. Some bricks and pipes come from clay. Beads and pieces of jewelry can come from clay too. Figures made from clay can be used in clay animation. You may have even played with modeling clay just for the fun of it!

Sand can be made into glass or bricks. It can also be put on a slippery road or sidewalk to help give you a better grip if you are walking or riding in a car.

Glass and bricks can be made from sand. Pottery and beads can be made from clay.

Using Resources For Energy

Plants need energy from the Sun. They use this to make food through photosynthesis. Solar energy reaches animals through the food chain. Animals get energy by eating plants or other animals.

People use energy in many ways. We use energy that comes from the food we eat. We use energy to light our homes, dry our clothes, and run our cars. One renewable energy source is solar energy. Sunlight heats the ground, which then heats the air. Wind energy comes from a cycle of heating and cooling air. Solar energy powers the water cycle by causing water to evaporate.

field of solar panels

Using Solar Energy

People have learned how to gather solar energy with solar cells. **Solar cells** can change solar energy into electricity. They can be used to operate devices such as calculators and hot water heaters. Many solar cells can be grouped together to form solar panels. Fields of solar panels can gather lots of energy, which can be changed into electric or heat energy.

Energy from Water

People also depend on moving water as a source of energy. Water that moves rapidly or drops from a higher location to a lower one, as in a waterfall, has great power. Dams are built in rivers so that the energy of the rushing water can be controlled. It can then be changed into electrical power.

This dam in the state of Washington controls the flow of water in the Columbia River.

Nonrenewable Resources

Nonrenewable resources are materials that are used faster than they can be replaced by nature. People make products and get energy from nonrenewable resources. Some energy-producing minerals are found in ores. An **ore** is a rock containing minerals that can be removed from Earth.

Fossil Fuels

Nonrenewable resources such as coal, natural gas, and oil are burned to create heat. They are called **fossil fuels** because they are made from organisms that lived long ago. Energy in fossil fuels came from the Sun.

Petroleum is another word for oil. Petroleum is formed from decaying sea organisms, such as fungi, plants, and bacteria. Energy stored in their bodies settled in the sea. Layers of sediment formed. Upper layers put pressure on lower layers. After millions of years, the pressure turned the remains into fossil fuels.

The dark layers of rock in this picture are coal. It is layered between other kinds of rock.

Mining Fossil Fuels

Mining fossil fuels can be dangerous for the environment. A great deal of petroleum is underneath the ocean. Getting this petroleum can be difficult.

The risk of an oil spill is one of the biggest concerns of drilling in the ocean. Oil spills can pollute the water. They can harm organisms living in the ocean. They can even cause problems for organisms that live on shore. Companies are looking for ways to make drilling less risky.

Even using fossil fuels can damage the environment. As fossil fuels burn, they can release harmful substances into the air. They may add carbon dioxide gas to the atmosphere. Too much carbon dioxide may lead to global warming. Pollution can also cause acid rain. When this acid rain falls, it can damage plants and animals.

This oil platform is drilling for oil deep beneath the ocean.

Making Resources Last

Nonrenewable resources are used for most of the world's energy needs. Fossil fuels are used up faster and faster as people use more and more energy.

Even renewable resources such as air, water, and soil are reduced when they are used wastefully or are destroyed. Restoring these resources and trying to reverse negative effects can be difficult. It is important not only to conserve energy, but also to use other sources of power.

Conserving Resources

Conservation is using only what you need without wasting it. People have already found ways to use fewer nonrenewable resources. Some people carpool, or ride together, to save gasoline. Others walk or ride bicycles. You can help by turning off lights you don't need and turning off the faucet as soon as you are finished. Companies are helping by making cars and appliances that use less energy.

Recycling

Many people are helping to use fewer nonrenewable resources by recycling used items. **Recycling** is saving, collecting, or using materials again instead of throwing them away. Many cities and towns have programs for recycling materials such as paper, plastic, aluminum, tin, and steel.

You can help your family, your school, and your community reuse and recycle metal, paper, and plastic. What you do today will help the world to have resources for years to come!

How many things can you recycle at home?

Glossary

conservation	the process of using only what you need without wasting it
fossil fuels	energy sources such as coal, oil, and natural gas that were made from organisms that lived long ago
humus	rich, dark brown, decomposing material that is part of soil
ore	rock containing minerals that can be removed from Earth
petroleum	the proper name for the fossil fuel commonly known as oil
recycling	the process of saving, collecting, or using materials again instead of throwing them away
solar cells	devices that can store energy from the Sun and change it to electrical or heat energy
solar energy	energy from the Sun